Purchasing Ethics

Peter L. Grieco, Jr.

PT Publications, Inc.
3109 45th Street, Suite 100
West Palm Beach, FL 33407-1915
(561) 687-0455

Library of Congress Cataloging in Publication Data

Grieco, Peter L., 1942-
    Purchasing ethics / Peter L. Grieco, Jr.
            p.   cm.
    Includes index.
    ISBN 0-945456-28-X
    1.   Purchasing—Moral and ethical aspects. 2. Industrial
procurement—Moral and ethical aspects.   I. Title.
HF5437.G473 1997
174'.4—dc21   97-30938
                                           CIP

TABLE OF CONTENTS

How to Use This Book

This book is designed to be used in conjunction with the corollary texts in our Purchasing Series. Please call us at the number below for more information about utilizing our tools. The idea behind this book is to read it with a pen in your hand so that you can answer the questions and write down the plans you are going to put into action. For those people who use this book alone, there is enough information to get you started on the road to excellence. Remember, however, that roadmaps such as this book are best accompanied by travel guides such as the ones we offer in the field of purchasing. Together, they can make your journey a rewarding one.

HELP DESK HOTLINE
1-800-547-4326

In order to answer the questions of our readers, we have established a Help Desk Hotline at our corporate headquarters in West Palm Beach, Florida. We invite you to call us with your queries about how to use the forms and tools in this book.

We also invite you to use our HELP DESK HOTLINE to find out more about other books we publish, as well as our *Supplier Surveys and Audits Forms* software and a videotape series entitled **Supplier Certification: The Path to Excellence**. In addition to books, software and videotapes, we offer over 80 courses which can be scheduled for intensive, in-house seminars. Call us for details.

ABOUT THE AUTHOR
Peter L. Grieco, Jr.

Peter L. Grieco, Jr., is a Partner with Deloitte & Touche Consulting Group, an international consulting and education firm specializing in the areas of Just-In-Time, Total Quality Control, Automation and Systems Implementation. He was active in the development of Apple Computer's Macintosh Automated Focus Factory in Fremont, California. His industry experience encompasses both repetitive and discrete manufacturing processes. He has more than twenty-five years of experience as a practitioner and educator in the manufacturing environment. He has held numerous operation and financial positions.

Mr. Grieco presently serves on the Stanford Research Institute Advisory Board (SRI) and is a member of the American Society for Quality Control (ASQC), the National Association of Purchasing Management, and the American Production and Inventory Control Society (APICS) where he has held positions as: Education and Research Foundation Director, National Secretary/Treasurer, Vice President of Region I (New England), and Past President of the Hartford chapter.

Mr. Grieco is the author of *Supplier Certification II: A Handbook for Achieving Excellence Through Continuous Improvement, World Class: Measuring Its Achievements, MRO Purchasing* and *Purchasing Ethics.* He is the coauthor of the latest JIT/TQC textbooks, *Made In America - The Total Business Concept, Just-In-Time Purchasing, Behind Bars: Bar Coding Principles and Applications,* and *The World of Nego-*

tiations: Never Being A Loser. He attended Central Connecticut State University and Wharton School of Finance (Moody's School of Commerce). He is a frequent lecturer for numerous professional societies, seminars, conferences, and numerous university programs on Operations Management and Just-In-Time/Total Quality Control related topics. He is also recognized in Inventory Management for his contribution to education and training.

PREFACE

Why should we be concerned with ethics? Why should we set standards for ethical behavior?

Consider this:

- Rarely does a person get fired after making a bad management decision. However, one ethical mistake often brings about termination of employment. Organizations are considerably less accepting of an ethical error than any other error in judgement.

- Ethics provide the rule we live by. One set of rules governs our business *and* personal lives. We have heard the refrain "That's business," as a way of rationalizing unethical business practices. However, unethical behavior in the business arena is not acceptable.

- A blemished public image resulting from unethical behavior hurts the organization. Customers who feel cheated will not continue to do business with the company and will not recommend the company to others. Consequently, some potential for new business is lost.

Purchasing professionals are constantly being examined. Therefore all actions must be above board, with no hint of indiscretion. Purchasing professionals should take pride in maintaining a standard of conduct that cannot be criticized.

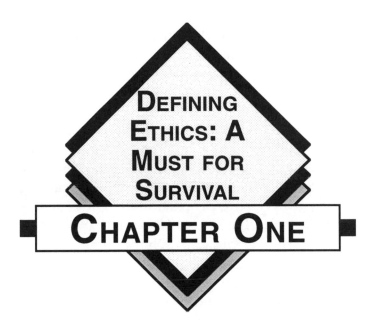

DEFINING
ETHICS: A
MUST FOR
SURVIVAL

CHAPTER ONE

Purchasing ethics is concerned with behavior, the rightness or wrongness of actions taken by a purchasing professional while pursuing the business goals of his or her organization. An organization will be generally defined in this book as a company, but it could also be a governmental department or agency, or a nonprofit institution. Although it is sometimes difficult to separate purchasing ethics from the ethics of the entire organization, we will mostly concentrate on the correct behavior in the purchasing function as purchasing personnel perform all activities dealing with the acquisition of goods and services in order for the company to produce a product or provide a service. What effects behaviors may have on society as a whole, although important, are beyond the scope of this book. We want to show the men and women working in the purchasing profession how and why the highest standards of conduct are central and necessary to the proper functioning, even survival, of a company.

Many companies subscribe to the standards of conduct promulgated by the National Association of Purchasing Management (NAPM). A brief discussion of each of its points reveals much about the ethical behavior required by purchasing professionals. The first standard says that the purchasing professional must "provide justice" to all the people with whom he has dealings. At its most basic level, this standard is simply a restating of the "Golden Rule": Do unto others as you would have them do unto you. The standard also makes it clear that you, as a purchasing professional, must not only act justly but correct any injustices that you come across. For example, it is not enough to provide accurate information to suppliers. A purchasing professional must also correct any inaccurate information that may have been inadvertently given to suppliers.

The second NAPM standard of conduct has two parts. The first part says that purchasing professionals must "buy without prejudice." This means that they cannot favor one source over another for any personal reason. They must be guided in their selection of suppliers by what is stated in the second part of the standard which says that they must seek "to obtain the maximum ultimate value" for the organization. The business goals of the company must come before any personal bias.

NAPM's third standard of conduct states that "honesty and truth" must be present in all purchasing activities. (Again, this must extend as well to the denunciation of "all forms and manifestations of commercial bribery.") Ethical purchasing professionals must go beyond the positive observance of these standards of conduct. You must be active in uncovering any breaches of conduct as well. As we shall see later in this book, management must take an active role in making ethical behavior part of the culture of the entire organization.

The fourth standard of conduct is concerned with obligation. The standard focuses on the upholding of promises that the purchasing professional makes to suppliers and the guaranteeing of the promises that suppliers make to the company. The purchasing professional is obligated to determine that all actions by all parties are consistent with good business practices. This, too, is an active role that does not end with the signing of agreements. The obligation to conduct purchasing activities in an ethical manner is a continuous one.

The last standard says that the purchasing professional should avoid "questionable or unethical practices." This is another way of applying the test of respectability, often expressed in one of these two ways: (1) Would your mother approve of what you are doing? (2) Would you want what you are doing reported on the front page of your local newspaper? If you answer "no" to either question, then you should probably avoid doing the activity. Another rule of thumb is that if you are not sure whether the practice is right or wrong, then chances are that it is a practice that you want to avoid becoming entangled in. Borderline areas in ethics are like foggy nights. You won't be able to see when you have crossed over the line between ethical and unethical.

Rate your purchasing department for each of these standards. Circle the number which best approximates where your department stands.

Justice

1	2	3	4	5
equal				unequal

Nonprejudicial

1	2	3	4	5
seeks company goals			seeks personal goals	

Honesty and Truth

1	2	3	4	5
completely scrupulous			will accept favors, bribes, and unauthorized gifts	

Obligation

1	2	3	4	5
consistent with good business practices			inconsistent with good business practices	

Avoidance

1	2	3	4	5
does not engage in questionable practices			engages in questionable business practices	

What can your company do, and what can you as a purchasing professional do, to improve your department's rating in each standard?

_____

_____

_____

_____

_____

Ethics as an Asset

Ethical behavior is unquestionably an asset to the company as a whole and to the individual working in the purchasing department of the company. First, let's consider how ethical behavior benefits a company. When ethical behavior is woven into the conduct of all the activities of a company, the result is an environment of trust and respect. Every worker from the highest to lowest levels knows that he or she will be treated fairly. This environment fosters two kinds of behaviors which are valuable to a company. The first behavior is the avoidance and uncovering of unethical practices which could result in costly legal entanglements or scandals which would turn customers away from the company. The second behavior is the fostering of a more creative and entrepreneurial spirit among workers who are no longer afraid of making mistakes which are essential to the growth of any company. This is borne out by the fact that most successful companies today were either not heard of twenty years ago or, if they had been around, were flexible enough to adapt to new market demands. The ethical company is in a far better position to adapt because its workers know that they do not have to fear losing their jobs or status if one of their experiments fails. We must remember that an environment of fear precludes almost all experimentation. Indeed, fear breeds avoidance which will spread to activities throughout the company. An unethical company is often an inefficient company. For this reason alone, ethics is a critical asset to an organization.

An ethical company also has far superior relationships with its customers and suppliers. Again, it is a matter of fairness. If a supplier knows that your purchasing department will always act above board, then that greatly increases the supplier's willingness to be open and honest with you. Furthermore, it makes it likely that this supplier will enter into a partnership with your company which will improve quality and lower total costs. Thus, ethical behavior leads to fruitful partnerships which will increase profits.

Ethical behavior is also an asset to the individual purchasing professional. Much of the buyer/supplier relationship is conducted on a personal level, so that an ethical buyer has a much better chance of establishing a strong rapport with his/her counterpart at the supplier. Personal integrity, in fact, is the most valuable asset buyers possess. This integrity means that buyers must follow a strict ethical code in all relations with suppliers. Purchasing professionals, at the very least, must never lie, cheat, steal, or appear to be doing so. For example, that means not making promises to suppliers that your company will buy large volumes of the supplier's product if you are given a lower price, when you have no idea whether or not this is what your company intends. It would also mean not withholding information from one supplier and providing it to another in order to influence a buying decision for personal gain. In addition, buyers should avoid all personal involvements that might reduce their objectivity. Too many dollars are at stake to risk a company's reputation, the quality of its products and services, or its productivity on the possibility of personal gain.

Does the ethics code of your purchasing department foster the creation of profitable partnerships with your suppliers?

_____

_____

_____

_____

_____

What is Ethics?

In many respects, ethics is far more important in today's purchasing environment than it has ever been in the past. Whereas before there were adversarial relationships between buyers and suppliers, today there are partnerships. Supply Chain Management is the reason behind this change, and it is a process which requires a high level of trust in order for the partnership to work to the mutual benefit of both parties. Trust, of course, is one of the cornerstones of ethics. As business partners, we behave ethically because we trust that others will behave ethically as well. This is not a blind faith. We trust that our suppliers will see that their own best ends will be met by their ethical behavior. Likewise, they trust that we will behave ethically because it is in our company's best interest to cooperate.

It is interesting to note that the sport which best describes this type of relationship in business is basketball, instead of the more traditional equating of business with football. Football is a team sport requiring each part to do precisely what is expected. Basketball is a much faster, more fluid game in which individual players have certain roles on the team. The difference between the two in business terms is this: basketball players act like partners who must react to constantly changing situations. Team members trust each other to play to the best of their individual ability. The same applies to business. As purchasing professionals, you know your suppliers are individual companies, but you also know that you will both have greater success if you build on a relationship of trust. In this type of environment, it would be unethical to let down a partner.

Ethics is also a preventative practice. Ethics means staying on top of the most current trends in purchasing and business. Often, ethical problems come up because people are in a new territory where there are no customs or standards, and where old customs and standards may not apply. For example, the business world has recently seen the advent of virtual corporations. In this new arena, alliances form and dissolve as quickly as needs arise and disappear. What does a partnership mean in this environment? It is common for two virtual corporations to be competing with each other today and becoming partners tomorrow. Clearly, loyalty and allegiance is not necessary in this new world of business, but just as clearly, the whole structure would fall apart without some level of trust and ethical behavior. As a purchasing professional, you must be aware of what is ethical and what is not in a number of new marketplaces. Lack of knowledge of what is unethical could lose your company a great deal of business.

The discussion above leads us to an area which we will discuss in much more detail in Chapter Four where we cover the importance of professional standards. And in Chapter Two, we will look at the relationship between personal, professional, and company ethics. In this introduction, we simply want to point out the need for purchasing professionals to work within their professional associations for the continuous improvement of ethical standards and the creation of new ones when that is necessary. Furthermore, all purchasing professionals should be actively engaged in educating themselves and others about their profession. It is often true that the latest advances in purchasing practices help eliminate opportunities for unethical behavior. And, as we have pointed out, it is sometimes true that advances can create new ethical problems. The responsible purchasing professional keeps abreast of these developments.

It must be kept in mind that the vast majority of business is conducted ethically. If it wasn't, there would not be the levels of economic activity we see today. People wouldn't trust each other enough to conduct any business. Another thought to keep in mind is that much unethical behavior is the result of ignorance of professional standards. There are, of course, people who will readily break laws and transgress standards to gain profit or advantage. Our advice is to avoid these people at all cost. In fact, it may prove much too costly to do business with them. Think of lawsuits, penalties, loss of reputation, and even prison. This brings up the tricky question of whistle-blowing, or reporting unethical behavior or people. This is an individual decision, but let us tell you a story about a reporter we know who wrote a series of newspaper stories about unethical and illegal activities at a state-run organization. The reporter's stories helped land one individual in jail. Some time after this person was locked up, he sent a letter to the reporter in which he *thanked* the reporter for stopping him from continuing his illegal activity.

Types of Purchasing People

The individual in the story above is probably typical of most people who undertake unethical activities. We call them the *Impressionable*. Often, they perceive some pressure in their life which causes them to choose unethical activities. This pressure can be due to personal or family circumstances, or it can be pressure to perform "no matter what" applied by the individual's supervisors or managers. The

Impressionable are not bad people. They are people who need guidance on the path of ethical conduct.

Then, there are the *Dishonest*. In our opinion, there is not much to say about people who break the trust of the people they work with or the suppliers they deal with. Our advice is simple and blunt: Weed them out!

Lastly, there are the *Honest*, the overwhelming majority who have no problem differentiating right from wrong. They are often forgotten or overlooked. This is a condition that a proactive ethics culture reinforces with rewards at times and always with a constant interaction between management and workers. As we shall see in Chapter Six, management should lead the way by making the ethical stance of the company clear to every employee.

What plans do you have to guide the *Impressionable*, weed out the *Dishonest*, and reinforce the *Honest*?

_____

_____

_____

_____

It is of course difficult to justify why Sales/Marketing provides free gifts, meals, and events, while purchasing professionals cannot receive them. We believe a strong code of standards for the company is required.

EXAMINING
THE THREE
LEVELS OF ETHICS

CHAPTER TWO

Part of the reason why it is difficult to distinguish right from wrong in many situations is that ethical behavior for the purchasing professional occurs at three levels simultaneously. Ethical decisions are made at the company level, at the level of the purchasing profession, and at the personal level. In this chapter, we are going to take a look at each level separately and at how the three interact. Let's give you a classic example. A good friend that you went to school with and have been friendly with ever since is moving to your town to work in the engineering department of one of your company's major suppliers. He will be working on the very family of products for which you are responsible for their procuring. You have always behaved ethically and you know that your friend has. What do you do in this situation to maintain the integrity of yourself, your profession, and your company?

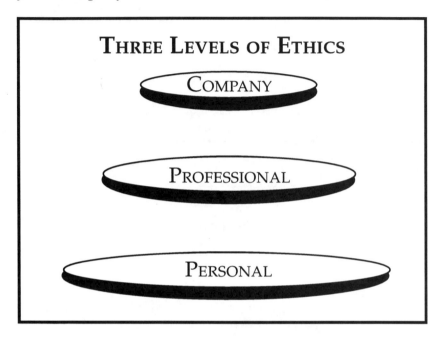

THREE LEVELS OF ETHICS

COMPANY

PROFESSIONAL

PERSONAL

This case would not present a dilemma if your company had clear guidelines and a consistent and fair code of ethics. Examining the three levels of ethics will help you and your company develop a code and culture in which integrity is maintained throughout the organization and in your company's relationships with other organizations. Let's look at ethics at the company and intercompany level.

The Company Level

As an ethical purchasing professional, you exist in the framework of the ethical behavior of your company.

What exactly does this mean? Most of us want to work for a company in which is not difficult for us to reflect the values of our employer. All companies, of course, operate in an environment that has been likened to a poker game. Each participant is acting for its own self-gain. If you own or manage a company, your business strategy depends on what you think other companies will do in the future. This is as true for your competitors as it is for your suppliers. At the same time you are gathering information on what other companies in the game are doing or what you think they may do, you are trying not to reveal your intentions. None of this behavior is considered unethical. The zero-sum, noncooperative style of business in which one company wins all without engaging in a strategy involving others is still a prevalent way of doing business. In today's business world, it may not always be the best business decision. This highly competitive and individualistic mode of operation can sometimes break down the networks of trust which exist between companies and within a company.

Relationships with Suppliers

Nowhere is this more true than in the relationship between your company and its suppliers. In the not too distant past, suppliers were treated in a hands-off manner. The purchasing professional was supposed to let market forces dictate which supplier received the order. This decision was based on quality, price and service. You were not allowed to make decisions based on personal interest or mutual back scratching. All of this is still true today, but a new set of market forces and worldwide competition in the global marketplace have changed the way we view our relationships with suppliers. This entails a high degree of cooperation and the sharing of much information and schedules. Some of these now common practices may have been considered unethical in past days; but playing fields change, and the players must adapt. The philosophy behind Supplier Management is that the cultivation of favored suppliers creates a situation where everybody involved gains. A motto for this process might be that a "rising tide floats all boats."

Setting Standards

Ethics is conforming to standards, and there are few institutions in our society that are more familiar with standards than business. In the business world, we have standards for quality, cost control, flexibility, financial reporting, and so on. The above definition of ethics thus fits very easily into the framework of how business is conducted. Ethics is one of the standards by which a company makes an economic decision. These ethical standards are set by looking to past company behavior, other companies, societal customs and the law. The idea is to make decisions that create the greatest good for the greatest number of people both within the company and in society at large. In other words, ethical business standards must take into consideration the results of the company's actions. Company leaders should set an example for all the employees of the organization. An ethical company not only sets standards of conduct but rigorously searches out unethical practices which would reflect badly on the company as a whole. As we shall see in Chapter Six, management has a company-wide role in setting ethical standards which improve the well-being of the entire work force.

The Professional Level

Just as your ethical behavior reflects upon the company for which you work, the same ethics reflect on your profession and its members. Traditionally, a profession has put an emphasis on the activities involved in providing a service or building a product, not on profit alone. A professional is more than someone with a certain amount of education and expertise. Professions also act as social entities which develop and enforce standards of behavior. In fact, one of the reasons why professions have become increasingly important in the business world is that there is a belief that if we all acted more professionally, there would be much less unethical behavior. The purpose of many business schools is to make business a profession so that ethics get defined as responsible professional behavior.

The rise of the professional class in business means that the loyalty of an individual to a particular company is supplemented by a loyalty to the profession and its ethical standards. Of course, one of the standards for all professionals, including purchasing professionals, is to do their best work for the company and not cooperate in unethical behavior which would reflect poorly on the company, the profession or the individual. This brings up the sticky situation in which the company's ethics are not up to the level of the profession. What do you, the ethical purchasing professional, do? The answer is not an easy one since you probably have obligations to your family and other people in your life. You could quit your job, but there are some who would argue that you should stay and use all of your influence and reasoning to convince your company that ethical behavior is the better business decision in the long run. Making the right decision in this situation is a tough call and ultimately a matter of your own personal ethics. One of your jobs as a purchasing professional is to work toward dispelling the notion that companies and business professionals must behave unethically at times in order to succeed and be profitable.

The Personal Level

For a purchasing professional, ethics at a personal level primarily comes into play in the form of pressures from external sources or conflicts of interest between the individual and the other two levels. Perhaps the most prevalent form of pressure is that which comes from superiors in the company demanding improved performance. In and of itself, this is, of course, not unethical. All companies should expect that their employees give the organization their best work. In fact, it would be unethical for a purchasing professional to do less than what the job requires. On the other hand, it would be unethical for a company to demand more effort and time from an employee than what is reasonable. People have private lives, and companies must not interfere with their employees enjoyment of their quality of life. Most of these situations are obvious to companies and their workers. The type of pressure from above that we are talking about is the insistence on improving performance no matter what. That could mean behaving unethically from a professional or personal level and in some cases even acting illegally.

This type of activity is wrong. Any company that asks this of its employees has no ethical standing whatsoever. It is not always so clear whether an employee with a mortgage, children going to college and aging parents has much of a choice. If such a worker cooperates in unethical behavior or turns a blind eye to it, then there is no mistaking that he or she has failed to sustain a high level of ethics. For people who find themselves in this situation, we suggest that you talk with trusted friends, the Human Resource Department, lawyers, clergy or your spouse about what you can do to rectify the situation if possible. Whistle-blowing is an option, too, but you must be careful here. Your resources usually will not match those of a company bent on covering up its unethical or illegal activities. Again, consult with those people that you trust about your course of action.

The situations we have just described come up when there is a conflict between levels of ethics. There is another type of conflict of interest in which you are called upon to make a decision for your company which could benefit you personally. For example, you may have bought some stock years ago in a company that is now being considered as a supplier. If you have the power as a purchasing professional to ensure that this supplier gets a large contract, you stand to gain a substantial amount of money when the value of the supplier's stock begins to rise. The ethical response to this dilemma is clear.

Remove yourself from making the decision. A longer-term answer is not to allow purchasing decisions to be made by one person acting alone. The supplier selection process that we describe in our book, *Supplier Certification II* (PT Publications, FL), will base purchasing decisions of this nature on objective standards. Once again, we see that setting standards is not only ethical, but sensible in terms of improved performance. The Big Five accounting firms have a restrictive standard in the employee hire agreement. An employee cannot own stock in an audit client. As an example: Deloitte & Touche audits many state lotteries, and employees cannot participate in those lotteries.

List three ways in which at least two of the levels of ethics discussed in this chapter interact in your role as a purchasing professional. Are there standards for any conflicts between the levels?

_____

_____

_____

_____

_____

THE
HEIGHTENING
INTEREST IN
ETHICS

CHAPTER THREE

Purchasing professionals have come a long way since this headline from the not-too-distant past appeared in a national newspaper: "All Purchasing Agents Are Crooks." As a result of actions by a few individuals and companies, the whole profession was being tarred with an undeserved bad reputation. This was the beginning of a heightened interest in ethics which led to professional standards being promulgated, maintained and continuously improved. Companies and individuals realized that it was bad for business when the public perceived the purchasing profession and all of business as disreputable. The interest in ethics today has become so strong that competitive companies are now vying to be perceived at the forefront of interest in health, community and environment. These are the ethical attributes that will distinguish your company from the competition.

Business Ethics

As we said, attitudes toward business have changed over the past thirty years. Polls in the mid-sixties indicated that more than half of the people in this country had strong confidence in the people who ran large companies. By 1974, this percentage had dropped to 21% and by 1976 to 16%. Another survey indicated that 70% of the public believed that companies fairly balanced profits with the public interest. By 1974, this figure had dropped to 20%. Public opinion came back in the 1980s, but then dropped again when businesses were perceived as greedy and the government as a bloated and inefficient purchaser.

The newspapers of that time ran countless stories of insider trading and sweetheart deals. The scandals surrounding Michael Milken of Drexel Burnham Lambert and John Gutfreund of Saloman Brothers were only the most familiar. But they brought up the ethical question, When does an entrepreneurial attitude and innovation cross the line into unethical behavior?

Companies were in the news as well. One food producer was charged with selling "apple juice" that had no real apple juice in it. This case resulted in fines and prison terms as well as unfavorable media attention and the erosion of the company's morale. This was a scenario repeated far too often across this country until people began to wake up and see the true costs of this behavior.

According to a TECHnotes publication of the National Association of Purchasing Management (NAPM), companies in the U.S. spent $7 billion on kickbacks and bribes in 1979. This number was estimated to have risen to $10 billion in 1988. As the publication points out, this meant that a company with a 5% return on sales had to earn twenty more dollars to cover each dollar in unethical purchasing activity.

Purchasing ethics also came into the limelight because many companies wanted to move their organizations from ones in which ethics was not an important concern to ones in which ethics was a primary concern. People asked how to introduce more ethical behavior into purchasing departments or how to raise present ethical levels, but they weren't sure how to implement new policies and structures or how to change existing ones. They needed to know then and still need to know what is right and why it is right. This is what we will extensively cover in the remaining chapters.

New demands and relationships with suppliers which were the result of companies adopting Just-In-Time and Supplier Certification also pushed the interest in purchasing ethics on to the center stage. But most of the heightened interest was due to scandals and confusion over what is ethical and unethical. For example, people were confused over what constituted a conflict of interest because they often hold divergent views. Individuals even have views which conflict with each other based on the situation. Consider the following list of statements about what ethical behavior consists of:

    1) Just follow traditional religious codes of behavior and you can't go wrong.

2) What is ethical? Everybody has their own set of beliefs.

3) There will always be unethical practices, but purchasing professionals are predominately ethical.

4) If I don't do what others do, my company won't be competitive, and I'll be out of a job.

5) Anything that is not illegal in the pursuit of profits is ethical.

There are honest people that would agree with some or all of these statements and honest people that would disagree with some or all of these statements. Judging what is ethical is not easy. There are no hard and fast rules. No black and white standards of behavior exist. That's why purchasing professionals are looking for answers. Hence, the interest in ethics.

Recent surveys of purchasing professionals conducted by NAPM have confirmed that there is an interest in improving codes of ethics. Although many companies have codes of ethics, the survey shows that they are not always complete. For example, slightly less than half of the codes have a procedure for implementing and administering the code. Only 37% contain sections about violations and discipline and only 13% cover back-door supplier calls. Clearly, there is room for more improvement.

Ethics of Dealing with the Government

The procurement problems at the Pentagon are only the tip of the government's problem in obtaining quality material at the lowest cost. The entire process of selecting suppliers and ensuring quality is riddled with outdated, inefficient and costly procedures. By focusing on products, such as hammers which cost $600, critics of government programs are falling into the same trap as the government. It is not the price and quality of products that the government should be concerned about, but the quality and control of processes at their suppliers' plants. Supplier certification is the only way the government can begin to address these issues as we point out in our Video Education Series ("*Supplier Certification: The Path to Excellence.*")

The first obstacle for the government to overcome is the entrenched bureaucracy present in most of its departments and agencies. Somebody in the executive branch, perhaps the President himself, has to take charge and make a commitment to ridding our government's procurement system of traditional and inefficient procedures. Once that commitment has been made, it is then necessary to educate and train an overworked and inadequately trained staff in the philosophy and application of supplier certification. This commitment to revamping procurement practices should pertain to all departments and agencies which purchase material for the government. In other words, there shouldn't be one system for the Department of Defense and another for the Food and Drug Administration. Part of the problem has been a sort of Tower of Babel approach to procurement by our government. Everybody speaks a different language. When a supplier to the government needs several "interpreters" to understand the mass of governmental regulations, then it should come as no surprise that costs escalate.

Anybody who has looked at government manuals issued to suppliers is aware of a plethora of paragraphs and subparagraphs stating procedures and specifications which must be adhered to. You would think by the sheer mass of information that the government is doing a good job of controlling every detail. By fixing their attention on the details, however, they have seen the trees, but missed the forest (These manuals fail to achieve quality at the supplier's plant because they emphasize picayune procedures over the control of processes.) The government has constructed a system which guarantees that suppliers will produce excellent paperwork *and* faulty components.

The government makes two mistakes when it formulates specifications for products. First, it draws up specifications for the inspection of finished products (rather than designing specifications for controlling a process.) Second, it overspecifies. Specifications are not determined by customer need. The government wrongly believes that by tightening specifications, it is ensuring quality. Quite the opposite is true. In a supplier certification environment, specifications conform to customer requirements. It seems, for example, that a soldier could get by with a $20 hammer off the shelf as well as he could with one costing 30 times more. There are, of course, some products that the government buys which require the most technically feasible specifications possible: parts for the space shuttle, for example. In other words, conformance to customer requirements varies according to the criticality of the part or material being purchased. Supplier certification recognizes this need and assures us of the highest quality and safety when this is truly the demand of the customer. The same criteria used for buying space shuttle parts, for example, need not be the same criteria we use to buy hammers or toilet seats.

These manuals, especially the MIL standards put out by the Department of Defense, are also oriented toward an Acceptable Quality Level (AQL) rather than a Certified Quality Level (CQL). As we have noted before, an AQL approach allows defects. In fact, a 2% AQL says that two parts out of every 100 will be bad. Total Quality

Control does not accept anything less than 100% quality and achieves that level by being statistically driven. There must be more emphasis in government documents of Statistical Process Control (SPC), a cornerstone of supplier certification.(With SPC, the emphasis is on controlling the supplier's process and making them responsible for producing quality parts.)If machines are so well maintained and controlled that they never produce bad parts, then 100% quality becomes a far easier goal to achieve as it eliminates wasteful paperwork and red tape. In fact, the government would find that far more suppliers would be willing to do work for the government if they did not have to jump through so many hoops.

The Packard Commission

Problems with purchasing practices in the defense industry and Pentagon became so widespread that during the Reagan era, a presidential commission headed by David Packard, chairman of Hewlett-Packard, was appointed to come up with guidelines on ethics in defense industry. The list below (from "Conduct and Accountability, A Report to the President's Blue Ribbon Commission on Defense Management," a public document that can be obtained at most university libraries) can be applied to all types of businesses.

1) Each company will have and adhere to a written code of business ethics and conduct.

2) The company's code establishes the high values expected of its employees and the standard by which they must judge their own conduct and

that of their organization; each company will train its employees concerning their personal responsibilities under the code.

3) Each company will create a free and open atmosphere that allows and encourages employees to report violations of the code to the company without fear of retribution for such reporting.

4) Each company has the obligation to self-govern by monitoring compliance with federal procurement laws and adopting procedures for voluntary disclosure of violations of federal procurement laws and corrective actions taken.

5) Each company has a responsibility to each of the other companies in the industry to live by standards of conduct that preserve the integrity of the defense industry.

6) Each company must have public accountability for its commitment to these principles.

Ethics in the International Arena

Because of the legal and logistical complexities, exchange rates and customs, government bureaus and departments, there are more chances that people will be able to gain from unethical practices in international procurement. The general lack of regulation often presents problems, but international trade is still based on trust and would fall apart if it wasn't mostly ethical. Many countries rely on treaties and trade agreements to make international trade easier and thus enhance its growth.

In the U.S., for example, we have made agreements such as GATT and NAFTA with our neighbors. Most people don't realize that GATT (General Agreement on Tariffs and Trade) has been around since 1948 and has been renegotiated seven times since the original agreement. The latest agreement (called the Uruguay Round) was negotiated "to create a predictable international trading field to transact business," according to Lee Krotseng in *Global Sourcing* (PT Publications, FL). Some of the provisions of the agreement reduce tariffs, protect intellectual property rights and extend the agreement to service companies.

Krotseng says that, "From a purchasing standpoint, it is too early to tell whether this latest round will be beneficial to all or to select industries (particularly since some provisions will not be implemented until 2005). In theory, new sources of supply will become available to the buyer creating new competition which will improve product innovation, quality, delivery and customer satisfaction."

Like GATT, the North American Free Trade Agreement (NAFTA), which currently covers Canada, Mexico, and the United States, was developed to make a level and fair playing field. Some of the objectives are also to reduce tariffs, protect intellectual property rights and extend the agreement to service companies. This agreement has been much more controversial in the U.S. Some say it will hurt industries while others say it help them. Whatever the case, we believe it can only help to enhance the ethics of procurement between the participating countries. Any agreement which increases the predictability of international trade is of great benefit.

Disadvantages and Risks of Buying Internationally

Many ethical problems arise out of different customs and language. The classic example is the Japanese use of "hai," meaning "yes." Westerners interpret this as agreement to the terms of a deal. The Japanese intend it as "Yes, I have heard you." Clearly, this difference in meaning can create bad feelings. We also need to be aware of the fact that our sense of ethics is not always the same as the sense of ethics in other cultures. Krotseng points out, for example, that "reciprocity is considered an integral part of doing business in Japan, while in the United States it may considered unethical or even illegal." Cultural differences also impact areas such as proprietary information, sexual harassment, nepotism, and child labor to name a few. Krotseng also notes, "Cultural differences can lead to misunderstandings." In the West, we prize individualism whereas cultures in the East value community. "This is one reason why," he says, "decision-making takes longer in Japan — all parties must reach agreement."

When sourcing internationally, purchasing professionals must remember these obstacles and traps and remember that what applies to one country doesn't necessarily apply to another. Each area is seen from a different point of view in different regions and countries. When determining your ethics standards for the international arena you must examine the factors, both positive and negative, existing in each location.

Lastly, when there are ethical difficulties in international procurement, it is not always easy to seek redress. There are international courts, but these are costly and often confusing. Most companies try to anticipate these issues and include them in their agreements. That is why it is important for companies to have their own written code of ethics to present to potential trading partners. The increase in international trading has brought about a concurrent interest in ethics issues involving companies from two different countries.

We advocate a team approach to international procurement in which people from Purchasing, Engineering, Marketing/Sales, Accounting, and top management consider the following factors:

1) Level of sophistication in foreign country's business community

2) "Practices of the trade" within the country

3) Economic system of the country – amount of government control

4) Localization issues

5) Cultural/internal issues

Business Ethics and Society

The effects of business on society present a number of ethical issues. Our experience is that problems of environment or good corporate citizenship are best solved in conjunction with the community in which a company operates. Businesses alone cannot find the best solutions. We need to work together. One thing that businesses can do, however, is be a World Class company. The best-run company is the company that does the best for its community. A good way to become World Class in terms of ethical responsibility to society is to strive to meet national standards.

MEETING
THE ETHICS
CHALLENGE

CHAPTER FOUR

A number of companies have paid attention to the heightened interest in purchasing ethics and have met the challenge of developing new methodologies for the procurement of goods and services. One of these companies is the Electric Boat Division of General Dynamics, one of the nation's two builders of nuclear submarines for the U.S. Navy. Like many defense contractors, Electric Boat faced some difficulties in the 1980s with cost overruns and inefficient operations. But that is now behind the company which was recently praised by the Navy Secretary as an example of what the defense industry can do when faced with the challenge of reforming purchasing operations. The Navy claims that Electric Boat's new system has already saved $500 million in design and preliminary procurements for the Navy's

---

new attack submarine while greatly enhancing the capability of the ship. Concurrent with the company's new procurement system is a new attitude by the Navy as well. The Navy Secretary has indicated that the Navy now seeks a new relationship with suppliers which is less adversarial. Teamwork has led to more productivity and innovation.

Professionalism and Ethics Go Hand-in-Hand

Ethics has also become the focus of a number of innovations at business schools across the country. Bill Daniels, who was instrumental in the development of the cable television industry, recently donated a total of $22 million in matching grants to help the Daniels College of Business at the University of Denver develop a state-of-the-art program. Besides focusing on the usual technical skills, the program also emphasizes ethics and professional behavior. Part of the money went to the establishment of the Institute for Professional Excellence (IPE), which stresses the values above and incorporates them into the business school's courses. For many, the reestablishment of ethics as central to the study of business echoes the call for professionalism which forms the motto for the Harvard Business School, which also received a very large draft.

TO MAKE BUSINESS A PROFESSION

We have always maintained that ethics and professionalism go hand-in-hand. This is evident in the basic definition of professionalism as a set of ethical codes and standards of practice. In the field of purchasing, there are a number of organizations which have written guidelines for standards of practice. Among this group are:

- **National Association of Purchasing Management**
- **Purchasing Management Association of Canada**
- **International Federation of Purchasing and Materials Management**
- **National Association of Educational Buyers**
- **National Contract Management Association**

Although many people equate ethics with legality or adherence to religious belief, it means much more in purchasing. Ethics begins with responsible professional behavior. Some of the qualities of a person engaging in this type of behavior include:

- **commitment to the maintenance of high standards.**
- **responsibility to the profession's image and integrity.**
- **service to the public good which the profession generates.**
- **ability to self-govern and self-regulate behavior in accordance with standards.**

An excellent example of how professional standards and individual ethics interact with the practice of business is the profession of accounting. Accounting's high standards of practice are based on government laws and regulations, but they go beyond this level to introduce self-governing and self-policing activities. The profession has developed professional standards for reliability, integrity and competence because it knows that it must have the confidence of its clients in order to obtain work and to do the work correctly. Professional standards in all types of businesses work to prevent unethical acts through the promulgation of guidelines, group socialization and disciplinary action when necessary. Clients see these procedures in place and know they will be treated fairly and honestly as well as obtain the highest level of service. In certain respects, you can look at professionalism as a quality control process.

The profession of purchasing has been working diligently to professionalize its activities. Much of this work began with a survey conducted in 1988 by Ernst & Whinney with NAPM's Center for Advanced Purchasing Studies, and cosponsored by *Purchasing World* magazine. A number of important findings were discovered. Here is an overview of some pertinent conclusions:

- There is not a solid degree of agreement yet on the best way to enforce ethical standards in the profession. Half of the people surveyed were in favor of having NAPM investigate and take action on complaints.

- Almost three-quarters of the companies surveyed have a written ethics policy.

- It has been proven that a formal ethics document and policy significantly lowers the level of unethical practices.

- Purchasing personnel have spent *less* time help-ing their companies determine ethical practices than in the past. We see this as an opportunity to step in and begin the vital process of self-governing.

An Ethics Code and How to Apply It

The purpose of an ethics code is to eliminate unethi-cal behavior by providing people with a clear idea of what their responsibilities are. The best way to apply an ethics code is to create one through a company-wide discussion of conduct and standards. If this process is coupled with education and training to get the word out and clarify concepts, you will have the best chance of making the code part of your company culture. And that is the aim.

The following are some examples of ethics codes. We begin with a statement which is typical of many institu-tions which subscribe to the National Association of Educational Buyers (NAEB):

- Purchasing Office personnel shall exercise sound business judgment and maintain the highest ethical and moral stan-dards in the conduct of college business. Personnel must discharge their duties impartially so as to assure fair and open competition between responsible contractors. More-over, they must conduct themselves in such a manner as to foster confidence in the integrity of the Purchasing Office.

- The college endorses the code of ethics as advocated by the National Association of Educational Buyers. Purchas-ing Office personnel are expected to be familiar with this code of ethics and abide by it.

The code they are referring to is the one followed by over 2000 colleges and universities. NAEB's mission is "to promote the development and use of sound purchasing management practices on campus." When a university or college worker is engaged in purchasing related activities, the following is the code they are asked to follow:

- Give first consideration to the objectives and policies of my institution.

- Strive to obtain the maximum value for each dollar of expenditure.

- Decline personal gifts or gratuities.

- Grant all competitive suppliers equal consideration insofar as state or federal statute and institutional policy permit.

- Conduct business with potential and current suppliers in an atmosphere of good faith, devoid of intentional misrepresentation.

- Demand honesty in sales representation whether offered through the medium of a verbal or written statement, an advertisement, or a sample of the product.

- Receive consent of originator of proprietary ideas and designs before using them for competitive purchasing purposes.

- Make every reasonable effort to negotiate an equitable and mutually agreeable settlement of any controversy with a supplier; and/or be willing to submit any major controversies to arbitration or other third party review, insofar as the established policies of my institution permit.

- Accord a prompt and courteous reception insofar as conditions permit to all who call on legitimate business missions.

- Cooperate with trade, industrial and professional associations, and with governmental and private agencies for the purposes of promoting and developing sound business methods.

- Foster fair, ethical and legal trade practices.

- Counsel and cooperate with NAEB members and promote a spirit of unity and a keen interest in professional growth among them.

National Association of Educational Buyers
Adopted July 1, 1985

The University of Texas subscribes to the same code. They also provide people with a number of brochures to navigate ethics laws and regulations. Here is a list of the publications they offer. Many of these topics would be helpful in your ethics process:

- "Ethics and the University of Texas System: A Brief Practical Guide" – a summary of the UT System Ethics Policy and guidelines for use of state resources

- "A Guide to Ethics Laws for State Officers and Employees" – prepared by the Texas Ethics Commission

- "UT Guidelines on Giving and Receiving Benefits" – information on how to avoid legal and/ or ethical problems

- "Can I Take It?" – also by the Texas Ethics Commission

In addition to these publications, the university also issues Ethics Advisory Opinions on a regular basis. Each paper addresses an ethics issue. The University of Texas also employs an Ethics Officer. Employees with questions about ethics laws or issues are encouraged to seek information. We think that all of these ideas which have been put into practice at the university help educate people about their responsibilities by making employees knowledgable about how laws, rules and policies are interpreted. Furthermore, we believe that these ideas are applicable to all types of organizations. The same can be said for the following purchasing procedures which are in place at East Carolina University.

- Exclusive responsibility for making all purchase contracts rests with the Materials Management Department.

- Competitive bids not required for procurements below $2,500. Department must still monitor for instances of abuse and ensure that the university is getting what it has paid for.

- Minimum of three quotes for procurements between $2,500 and $5,000.

- Procurements over $5,000 must go through formal Purchase and Contract process performed by Materials Management.

- Standing Order Charge Cards are only issued to university employees and student assistants. Card holder is responsible for all charges.

Here is another set of useful guidelines used by the state government of Virginia. There is an ethics section of the Virginia Public Procurement Act (VPPA) which tells public employees how they should proceed when procuring items or services in their official capacities. Section 11-74 of the Code of Virginia states:

"...no public employee having official responsibility for a procurement transaction shall participate in that transaction on behalf of the public body when the employee knows that:

1. The employee is contemporaneously employed by a bidder, offeror or contractor involved in the procurement transaction; or

2. The employee, the employee's partner, or any member of the employee's immediate family holds a position with a bidder, offeror or contractor such as an officer, director, trustee, partner or the like, or is employed in a capacity involving personal and substantial participation in the procurement transaction, or owns or controls an interest of more than five percent; or

3. The employee, the employee's partner, or any member of the employee's immediate family has a pecuniary interest arising from the procurement transaction; or

4. The employee, the employee's partner, or any member of the employee's immediate family is negotiating, or has an arrangement concerning, prospective employment with a bidder, offeror or contractor."

The code then states that public employees cannot accept or solicit gifts from bidders, offerors, contractors, or subcontractors. At the web site for Virginia Tech's Purchasing Department which abides by the act above, they also spell out what the punishment can be for a public employee who violates the Ethics section.

"Willful violation of any provision of the Ethics section of the Act constitutes a Class I Misdemeanor. Upon conviction, any public employee, in addition to any other fine or penalty provided by law, shall forfeit his/her employment."

The site also provides useful definitions of the terms used in the ethics section so that there will be no confusion by what is meant. Listed below are three definitions which are useful in any organizational setting:

Immediate family — "a spouse, children, parents, brothers, sisters, and any other person living in the same household as the employee."

Official responsibility — "administrative or operating authority, whether intermediate or final, to initiate, approve, disapprove or otherwise affect a procurement, or any claim resulting therefrom."

Procurement transactions — "all functions that pertain to the obtaining of any goods, services or construction, including description of requirements, selection and solicitation of sources, preparation and award of contract, and all phases of contract administration."

While we are discussing government ethics, we think that everybody would do well to adopt the code used by the city of Broken Arrow, Oklahoma. Here are the rules that they require themselves, as well as their suppliers and contractors, to follow.

PURCHASING ETHICS

- "First consideration shall be given to the objectives and policies of the System and its components institutions. Every effort shall be made to obtain the maximum ultimate value for each dollar of expenditure. Honesty in sales representation shall be demanded, whether offered through the medium of oral or written statement, an advertisement, or a sample of the product.

- The Purchasing Agent and his staff and others authorized by or under these regulations to make purchases shall not accept personal gifts or gratuities that might in any way result in an obligation (real or personal) to individuals or firms seeking business.

- All qualified, reputable bidders shall be given equal opportunity to submit bids on a uniform basis when competition is possible. No bidder shall receive special consideration or be allowed to revise a bid after the time set for receiving bids. Any violations of these purchasing ethics shall be reported promptly to the Purchasing Agent."

It has been our experience that codes of ethics are not effective if they are seen as mere rhetoric. The question then becomes how to make the codes into something other than what people pay lip service to. We will go into this in much more detail in Chapter Six where we discuss the role of management in ethics. But, to put it simply, the most effective way to make sure ethics codes are believed and followed is to make what they say part of your company's culture. Ethics should be part of the basic processes of your company, including relationships with employees and suppliers as well as customers. Codes work best when they reinforce ethical practices, not when they try to create them. This is why there must be management commitment. Other necessities for a code are that it be relevant to the potential ethical problems of a particular industry, that it be promulgated to the entire company and that it shows how people are held accountable.

At their most basic, codes of ethics show where ethical problems may arise and how to avoid them. It is better, in most cases, if they are both prescriptive and proscriptive, that is, they should tell workers what to do as well as what not to do. Their primary purpose, however, should be to instill a sense of responsibility and accountability that is in tandem with the company culture. We have found that a good way to keep the code fresh in people's mind is to periodically challenge and evaluate every phrase and word in the document. This gets people involved so that they feel they have helped to make the rules by which they work.

Company Policy and Ethics

Although there are differences of opinion over how detailed a company's policies and procedures should be, we believe that part of your company's manual should contain policies defining the responsibilities of your purchasing department with respect to ethics. Furthermore, there is a need for these guidelines to be consistent for both the purchasing and sales departments when it comes to the following items:

- Gifts

- Entertainment

- Back-door selling

- Market intelligence

Your company's manual should also contain a policy for the handling of competitive bids. It would be important to consider as well the potential for problems arising out of the handling of presale technical services or in the purchasing of design services. In other words, every company's ethics policy will be different. To give you a foundation upon which to build your company's policy, we have provided the following checklist. (Some of the items in this checklist will be covered in the next chapter on the legal considerations of ethics.)

Do you have a written company policy in place for_____?

	YES	NO
• Gifts	____	____
• Reciprocity	____	____
• Disclosure statements	____	____
• Competition	____	____
• Contractual relationships	____	____
• Preferential treatment	____	____
• Meals	____	____
• Trips	____	____
• Confidentiality of information	____	____

Regardless of the level of detail you include in your policies and procedures, you cannot let them stagnate. You must monitor your ethics program on an ongoing basis to keep up with today's dynamic business environment. Factors which can affect your ethics program include:

- business expansion, especially global.

- state and federal laws – new or revised.

- new technology.

Suppliers and Our Special Responsibility to Them

We've left the discussion of suppliers for last because of the important relationship that exists between your company and company's which supply you the goods and services you need to conduct business. In a supplier partnership relationship, the buying company often places personnel with the supplier to assess and improve manufacturing processes. This obviously puts an increased emphasis on keeping information about a supplier confidential. Likewise, you need to inform your suppliers of developments which may substantially alter the quantities of materials or services that you buy. Since you are in a long-term partnership with certified suppliers, you need to consider their expectation of continued business. Many companies feel that they have an obligation to prepare suppliers for the eventual cessation of buying when a product reaches the end of its life cycle. At the very least, you must be fair and not leave suppliers in a position that threatens their survival. In addition to the above, here are some more areas which you will need to pay particular attention to:

- Back-door selling
- Price disclosure
- Bidding
- Negotiations
- Entertainment
- Gifts

These items should be spelled out in a Supplier Partnership Agreement which details the responsibilities of both the buyer and the supplier in the certification process. It is not a purchase order. It works in conjunction with purchasing agreements, blanket orders or system contracts. Instead, it is a mutually developed document which provides that the supplier delivers goods or services which conform to requirements 100% of the time. Its purpose is to state responsibilities before the product is made or the service is provided and to create an understanding of the working relationship.

The Contents of a Supplier Partnership Agreement

The agreement's purpose is to map out how the customer and the supplier will integrate all of the issues discussed in this chapter. It will contain a statement of purpose and scope and set objectives:

Terms and Conditions

- Sets quantity levels for raw material, work-in-process, assemblies or services which reflect flexible production schedules

- Defines quality level as zero-defects

- Controls price fluctuations and conditions for cost/price changes

- Establishes delivery schedules and windows as well as shipping terms and packaging specifications

- Defines terms of payment

- Establishes responsibilities for corrective action in the event of nonconformance

In order to have a true partnership, each side must be committed to meeting certain responsibilities. This is the core of any successful agreement. Neither side should feel as though they are being taken advantage of. It is important to stress that a partnership must achieve:

- 100% quality.
- 100% delivery.
- 100% quantity.
- 100% of the time.

The chart on the following page illustrates some of the responsibilities of both partners.

In the next chapter, we will turn our discussion to a concentration on the legal aspects of purchasing ethics. They, too, are part of the ethics challenge that we must face in our striving for the highest levels of professionalism.

RESPONSIBILITIES OF A SUPPLIER PARTNERSHIP

	MANUFACTURER	SUPPLIER
1.	Process-achievable specifications	Evaluate process capability to meet customer specifications
2	Clear standards – quality, quantity, and delivery	Evaluate standards/methods
3.	Clear line of communication	Clear line of communication
4.	Notification of organizational changes	Notification of organizational changes
5.	Discussion of potential changes in requirements	Discussion of potential changes in requirements and improvement
6.	Assist supplier in solving quality, production problems	Notify customer of quality, production problems and capacity
7.	Provide timely feedback and corrective action	Provide timely feedback and corrective action
8.	Provide audit schedule	Notify customer of sourcing process changes
9.	Share audit results	Close feedback loop
10.	Resolve supplier questions	Inform customer of new process and/or materials (partner)
11.	Commit to continuous improvement program	Commit to continuous improvement program

Figure 4.1

LEGAL
CONSIDERATIONS
OF ETHICS

CHAPTER FIVE

The legal consideration of ethics covers a large territory which would include contractual relationships, personal purchases, as well as conflicts of interest, disclosure and reciprocity. We are going to concentrate on the latter grouping in this chapter. One obvious reason why we study legal questions with regard to ethics is to avoid situations which could result in fines and even jail for serious infractions. Furthermore, engaging in illegal activities opens a company up to threats of being exposed. This makes it difficult for a company who has compromised its integrity to stop dealing with a supplier. Such a company may find itself facing a situation of economic blackmail in which a relationship with a supplier must be continued even though there are better suppliers from which to procure goods and services. The following

---

discussion will guide you so that these unethical situations never arise among your company's purchasing department and employees.

Conflicts of Interest

Conflicts of interest is the area that most commonly comes to mind when discussing purchasing ethics. The standard example given is that of a company employee having a financial stake in the firm of a supplier. Such an employee has the potential ability to manipulate purchasing decisions so that the supplier obtains more business. This employee would then benefit from the increased profits of the supplier and opens himself or herself to illegal bribes and kickbacks. The temptation is always present in such a situation for unethical behavior. In addition to potential illegalities, there is the question of whether the employee is making the most sound business decision. The supplier may not be the best choice because it may not represent the lowest total cost and highest quality levels. For these reasons, companies have developed policies concerning conflicts of interest. Here is a simple definition and a list of areas or activities to avoid being involved in a conflict of interest.

> **Conflict of Interest** – Employees and officers must refrain from private business or professional activities that may conflict, or appear to conflict, with the interests of the company and must refrain from using, or appearing to use, their position for personal gain.

> Ask yourself these questions to help you decide

if there is a conflict of interest:

- Do my personal concerns and my company's concerns conflict or appear to conflict?

- Does this situation improperly influence a person's decision-making process?

- Are decisions "for sale" or appear to be "for sale"?

Any employee who believes that he or she faces a conflict of interest should discuss the situation with his or her supervisor.

Activities to be avoided:

- Working for or investing in a competitor, supplier or customer

- Engaging in an activity or working for another company so as to encroach upon fulfilling the terms of your employment

- Lending or borrowing money from a customer or supplier

- Doing business with a company owned or controlled by a family member

- Accepting gifts, gratuities, favors, services or compensation from a customer or supplier beyond what is considered an acceptable business practice

- Using inside information to buy or sell securities

Disclosure and
Data Confidentiality Agreements

The Data Confidentiality Agreement is a document designed to be used with a supplier when it is necessary to "disclose, furnish or exchange data in which the disclosing party identifies a proprietary interest or a desire for confidentiality... The agreement establishes the rights and obligations regarding such proprietary interests and confidentiality and procedures for handling and protecting the data." Some of the items which a company may wish to protect include information about price and cost, product design, process, business plans, assets, wages and salaries, and personnel records. The document covers a number of areas, such as:

- termination date of agreement.

- continuing effectivity of the provisions of the agreement regarding confidentiality to any data remaining in receiving party's possession after the agreement terminates (when appropriate).

- destruction of data by receiving party and written certification of destruction to disclosing party, or return of all data to disclosing party.

- restriction on disclosure to third parties.

- restrictions on use by receiving party.

- procedure in the event of legal action.

In the agreement, the company makes it clear that any confidentiality agreement binds the whole company and all its elements. That is why it is necessary to carefully draw up the document so that the restrictions "do not interfere with the normal operations of other parts of the corporation." The following is a confidential agreement that we were asked to sign by a client. We thought it was a good example to include in this book.

AGREEMENT OF CONFIDENTIALITY

This agreement made and entered into as of the _____ day of _____ by and between The Company, a corporation with offices in _____ and (Name of supplier).

WITNESS THAT:

WHEREAS, both parties for their mutual benefit, anticipate the possible need to disclose to and receive from the other party, from time to time, information which the furnishing party considers to be proprietary and which relate to the Supplier Certification Program (hereinafter called "Program").

NOW THEREFORE, _____ and _____ do hereby mutually agree as follows:

1. MARKING OF INFORMATION
Any information exchanged by the parties and entitled to protection hereunder shall be identified as such by an appropriate stamp or marking on each document exchanged designating that the information is "Proprietary," and if oral disclosure of such protectable data is made, such data shall be so identified at time of disclosure. Within thirty (30) days thereafter a written notice with complete summaries of all oral disclosures desired to be protected, appropriately stamped or marked, shall be delivered to the receiving party addressed as noted hereafter in this Agreement. Transmittal of documents exchanged shall be evidenced by written notice from the disclosing to the receiving party.

2.   PROTECTION AND USE

The receiving party shall hold each item of proprietary information so received in confidence until ___ years after the expiration of this Agreement. During such period the receiving party shall use such information only in connection with the purpose of this Agreement and shall make such information available only to its employees having a "need to know" with respect to said purpose. In connection therewith the parties shall advise each such employee of obligations under this Agreement. Except when authorized in writing by the disclosing party, the receiving party shall not otherwise use or disclose such information during the aforesaid period, except that it may without the other party's consent be disclosed by the receiving party to the cognizant U.S. Government agency in connection with proposals related to the Program; provided, however, that any such disclosure bears the restrictive legend as applicable of FAR 15.509, Use and Disclosure of Data, or FAR 52.215-12, Restrictions on Disclosure and Use of Data in effect on the effective date of this Agreement, or a successor provision substantially the same. No data provided under this agreement shall be delivered under a contract or otherwise made subject to a contract "rights of data" clause.

Neither party hereto shall, without the prior written consent of the other, use in whole or in part proprietary information disclosed by the other to manufacture or enable manufacture by third parties of the disclosing party's products, products similar thereto, or products derived therefrom. The disclosed information and all copies thereof shall, upon the expiration or termination of this Agreement, be returned to the respective party, or be destroyed and a written certificate of destruction shall be provided to the disclosing party.

3.   EXCLUSIONS FROM PROTECTION

Information shall not be afforded the protection of this Agreement if, on the effective date hereof, such data was or subsequent hereto that such data is:

(a) developed by the receiving party independently of the disclosing party; or

(b) rightfully obtained without restriction by the receiving party from a third party; or

(c) publicly available other than through the fault or negligence of the receiving party; or

(d) released without restriction by the disclosing party to anyone including the United States Government; or

(e) known to the receiving party at the time of its disclosure.

4.   LEGAL ACTIONS AND GOVERNMENT REGULATIONS

Should the receiving party be faced with legal action or a requirement under U.S. Government regulations to disclose information received hereunder, the receiving party shall forthwith notify the disclosing party, and upon the request of the latter, the receiving party shall cooperate in contesting such disclosure. Except in connection with a failure to discharge the responsibilities set forth in the preceding sentence, neither party shall be liable in any way for any disclosures made pursuant to judicial action or U.S. Government regulations, or for inadvertent disclosure where the customary degree or care has been exercised by the receiving party as it normally uses to protect its own proprietary or confidential information; provided that upon discovery of such inadvertent disclosure or use it shall have notified the disclosing party and shall have endeavored to prevent any further inadvertent disclosure or use.

5.   NO RIGHTS GRANTED

Nothing in this agreement shall be construed as

granting or conferring any rights on the part of either party by license or otherwise, expressly or implied, to any invention or discovery or to any patent covering such invention or discovery.

6.   INDEPENDENT CONTRACTOR
Each party in undertaking its responsibilities hereunder shall be deemed an independent contractor and nothing in this Agreement shall constitute, create, or in any way be interpreted as a joint venture, partnership, or formal business organization of any kind.

7.   TRANSMISSION AND CONTROL POINTS
The exclusive points of contract with respect to the transmission and control of information furnished by either party to the other hereunder shall be as follows:

(Name and address of other party)

(Name and address of the Company)

Either party may change the above points of contract at any time providing written notification to the other party.

8.   EXPIRATION/TERMINATION
This Agreement shall expire _____ year(s) after the day and year first above written except that it may be terminated earlier by 30 days prior written notification of either party to the other or extended by mutual agreement. The provisions of paragraph 2 above shall survive such expiration or termination.

IN WITNESS WHEREOF, the parties hereto have caused this agreement to be duly executed and in effect on the day and year first above written.

```
Your Company          Name of other party
By: _____  By: _____
Title: _____    Title: _____
```

ACCEPTANCE
```
Supplier Signature:
Title:
Company Supplier Code:
    Procurement Manager:
    Procurement Quality Assurance Manager:
    Manufacturing Engineering Manager:
    Controller:
```

Reciprocity and Antitrust Laws

As a purchasing professional, you need to be familiar with antitrust laws in order to avoid reciprocity which is an agreement which restrains competition. For example, a company gives preference to a supplier who is also a customer. If the supplier is the best source, there is no problem. But if the supplier is chosen over other suppliers who deliver goods or provide services at a lower total cost, then there are ethical and even legal problems. The intent of antitrust laws is to provide a level playing field for all companies. Reciprocity can create situations in which one company receives unfair advantages. If this is allowed to happen, it will substantially weaken the credibility of your company in the marketplace. All purchasing decisions should be based on lowest total cost, quality and delivery. Any other factors are either unethical or give the appearance of being unethical and, in some instances, the consideration of other factors is illegal.

We advise companies to include strong and clear language in their policies of ethics codes that opposes reciprocity. There are four applicable federal acts which you need to know. In addition to being familiar with this antitrust legislation, we also strongly advise consulting a lawyer whenever there is a possibility of reciprocity.

- **Sherman Antitrust Act** — Passed by Congress in 1890, it prohibits contracts, conspiracies (such as price-fixing) or combinations which act in restraint of trade or attempt to monopolize any part of interstate trade.

- **Clayton Act** — Passed in 1914, it prohibits price discrimination between different buyers where the effect is substantially to lessen competition or tend to create a monopoly in any line of business. It bans monopoly-like "tie-in" arrangements, such as requiring the purchase of two items at the same time and refusing to sell them separately.

- **Federal Trade Commission Act** — Passed in 1914, it gives the commission power to issue cease and desist orders and to set up the General Trade Commission. This act prohibits unfair methods of competition and other inequitable or misleading activities.

- **Robinson Patman Act** — An amendment to the Clayton Act of 1914, it prohibits both direct and indirect discrimination in price as well as in services and allowances of life, grade and quality.

It should be noted, however, that ethical behavior

goes beyond just obeying the law. Many actions that are unethical, like taking advantage of trust, are not illegal.

Over the past few chapters, we have looked at some specific areas in purchasing ethics. This study will only bear fruit in your company through the efforts of management. In the next chapter, we explore the role of management and how it can instill ethical behavior into the purchasing function.

ROLE OF MANAGEMENT IN ETHICS

CHAPTER SIX

One of the first things that management can do in the area of purchasing ethics is recognize that fear often generates unethical behavior. The pressure of the bottom line often induces people to cut corners in order to make those monthly numbers. We are not saying that there should be no monthly numbers to meet. What we are saying is that if people need to go outside the rules to meet these numbers, then the problem is a company-wide one. A consistent inability to achieve the proper performance levels is most often the result of poor management. In the well-run company, there is less pressure because these goals are usually met. Thus, there is less cutting of corners and possibility for unethical behavior.

But, of course, ethics is much more than meeting the bare minimum of requirements. An ethics program that has become part of the company culture has many more benefits. Some of the changes and rewards that your company will experience are listed here:

- An increased sense of personal pride and satisfaction exhibited by all employees

- No costly legal entanglements resulting from questionable behavior

- No scandals which would adversely affect business

- Better relations with customers and suppliers

- More creativity and entrepreneurial spirit as a result of a free and open business environment

Corporate America is not alone in the challenges of implementing an ethics program. As the federal government investigations into health care fraud continue, hospitals nationwide are examining the way they do business. Columbia/HCA Healthcare, facing an extensive investigation into Medicare fraud, announced in October 1997 that it hired an "ethics expert" to administer its ethics compliance program, formerly managed by an assistant to Columbia's general counsel.

According to the *USA Today* article, Alan Yuspeh, who has counseled the defense industry since the '80s when the Pentagon overbilling scandals made headlines, was appointed as Columbia's senior vice president of ethics, compliance and corporate responsibility. He plans to focus on the future, down-playing Columbia's past behavior. With his team, he anticipates the creation of "a corporate culture where Columbia workers feel compelled to do what is right." Among his first goals are to "... boost workers' training in compliance, develop a code of conduct for employees and create an internal mechanism for worker's to report any wrongdoing."

This is just the beginning. Just as many corporations still do not have complete ethics programs, the health care arena also has a long way to go. Can you believe that only 5% of the 5400 hospitals and medical schools in the United States have a comprehensive ethics compliance program?

Benchmarking as an Ethics Tool

A brief overview of how to use a benchmarking process requires that we adapt the ethics methods from others to our program. Each company faces a unique set of ethical problems as we pointed out earlier in this book. Even with that warning, we think that benchmarking the ethical programs of successful companies with a reputation for being ethical is the best place to begin your own process of instilling ethics in your company.

Benchmarking is used to identify those companies who already excel at ethics. The use of benchmarking allows you to form or improve upon your own company's ethics program by taking certain practices from Company X and another set of practices from Company Y and applying them. Benchmarking is intended to provide opportunities to eliminate risk and make breakthrough

BENCHMARKING TEAM MEMBER CHECKLIST

	POSSIBLE POINTS	SCORE
• Skills in area to be benchmarked	20	
• Understands processes and measurements	10	
• Trained in benchmarking	15	
• Understands team dynamics	10	
• Able to "clone" idea in other areas	10	
• Known and respected in organization	8	
• Trained in problem solving	20	
• Able to perform cost analyses	7	
TOTAL	100	

improvements. The idea is to use the best of the best in creating your ethics process.

There is always some organization you can learn from and that company may be in an industry totally unrelated to your own. The point of benchmarking is not simply to point out differences, but to determine why they exist. The guidelines below will help you begin benchmarking at your company:

1) Identify all ethics areas to be benchmarked.

2) Identify the correct ethics benchmarking partners.

3) Research sources of information on best-in-class ethics practices.

4) Perform ethics gap analysis on information obtained.

5) Plan strategies and tactics to close the ethical gap.

6) Set objectives for your ethics plan.

7) Implement your ethics plan.

Ethics and Company Culture

In order to be fully effective, ethics must be an everyday concern which becomes part of your whole company's culture. You need to bring ethics to the foreground through a direct, hands-on approach. Among other strategies, this would include the dissemination of company culture through anecdotes and leading by practicing what you preach. Another excellent course of action is to coach junior employees and to allow them unconditional access to upper management on ethical issues.

Culture change is always difficult for an organization, but we have developed a process which has proved successful in a number of different types of organizations. (See *People Empowerment: Achieving Success from Involvement* (PT Publications, FL) for a complete discussion of this topic.) Here are some of the required changes that we think need to happen.

A company must adopt proactive rather than reactive management philosophies and create an atmosphere of trust where people are empowered and involved ethically. A culture based on ethics must be one in which people feel free to take the initiative in approaching upper management with problems and ideas for solving them. An "open-ear" policy is an integral part of this new environment. We say "open-ear" because an "open-door" policy often doesn't have the desired result of producing a policy of listening. In fact, the eventual outcome of this new culture is to have people who are self-governing. They know what is ethical and what is not. And when there is any question, they know when to turn to management whose primary job is to be an internal "consultant" on ethical issues. It will probably be necessary to evaluate present organizational structures in order to promote this policy. People need to feel that management has given them the authority, responsibility and resources to put their ideas into action.

Recently we were involved with the discharge of a very good employee who was found to have misrepresented herself on her employment application. In this situation, would you maintain and trust a person who has financial responsibilities, keys to the company and can spend company money? These are not easy decisions to make or follow-up on.

What are the common ingredients of those companies which have been able to implement successful ethics programs? From our experience in the field, we have been able to isolate four factors:

1 **The commitment of top management.** This is

where the formulation of a vision must start. That vision must be driven by the marketplace in concert with the strategic plan.

2 **Total participation of management.** Never, never, expect people to engage in a process of which you aren't willing to take part. Management must realize that they are a service organization for the employees.

3 **Participation by people.** The old days of "us" and "them" are over. The people who work at a company are every bit as important as management. They should be listened to. Listening is one of the steps used in gaining participation.

4 **Continuous improvement teams.** This is the grass-roots action level of ethics programs. Without teams, the process will become a management-only program. As we have found out in the past, such programs are never as effective as ones that are activated by people.

One effective way to help people become aware of a company's vision on ethics is to allow them to participate in the development of statements which convey the mission of both the company and its people. The involvement in the development of the vision acts as a motivator in making ethics the primary responsibility of all people.

Education and Training in Ethics

Training and education is another effective method for indoctrinating people into a company culture pervaded by a strong sense of ethics. Education is learning the theory behind what you are doing; training is putting into practice what you have learned. Educating and training people about ethics must occur at all levels of your organization. The goal is to provide a positive environment which will stimulate people to openly discuss ethical issues. In other words, training and education must also become a way of life in your company. Below are some of the methods we advocate in developing a keen ethical sense in your company:

- Set clear guidelines and standards.
- Support conditions which reinforce ethical behavior.
- Develop a system of rewards and punishments.

Both management and senior executives must be involved in company education and training and set the example. Socializing at company events and gatherings between the different levels creates feelings of responsibility to company as well as a strong desire to do what is right for the company. Trust develops and leads to an attitude in which people don't want to let the group down.

We also advise that education and training in ethics should allow a lot of time for case studies and questions. There should be far more than ten minutes of group discussion after a one-hour presentation on a purchasing ethics topic. In fact, the ratio may work better if it was reversed. Also remember to focus on what is relevant to the group being addressed. Use case studies to begin discussions of ethical problems specific to your company or industry. Since specific examples are more relevant, they are far more likely to be heard and retained by employees. Your job is not to simply lecture about your company's ethics policy, but to find ways to discuss ethics. This is the most effective way to make ethics part of your company's culture.

General Management Guidelines

The paramount guideline when it comes to the role of management in ethics is to set clear objectives. You must be absolutely clear about what you want to happen. One of the ways that you can find out what to include in your ethics program is through internal research and background checks on people who want to work for the company. In the next chapter, we will cover how to design and implement a company survey. Surveys are part of the process of getting people to buy into the program. So is the granting of responsibility and authority to all levels of the company. An involved and empowered worker has a stake in the company. The role of workers and management is to create more than just rules, but to find ways to reduce pressures which can lead to unethical practices. This is best accomplished by defining roles carefully and by giving your staff adequate support, allotting them enough time to finish tasks, and involving senior management in all facets of the program.

We can't emphasize enough that you need to make ethics a constant concern. Next in importance is to fit your approach to your organization. Look for ways to exploit current company practices in order to reinforce your ethics program. Quality programs, for example, are often an excellent gateway for introducing people to the necessity of allowing issues to come to the surface. The surfacing of issues before they become problems means the program is working well. Just like Just-In-Time, your ethics program should expose issues so that they can be solved. Teams are an important part of this process as we shall see in the next chapter.

One of the companies we worked with in 15 European countries had some ethical discussions that need to be shared. We were talking about receiving gifts from suppliers when someone from the French delegation said, "Receiving good vintage French wine is okay, is it not?" Now, are we talking about just one bottle or a full case? Are we addressing the business of buying work or a courting practice? It is important and expected in some Asian countries to present a token gift when first meeting. What we need is a policy with a dollar value established for both giving and receiving.

THE
HUMAN FACTOR
IN ETHICS

CHAPTER SEVEN

All of our discussion about purchasing ethics eventually comes to this point: how to deal with the individual employee's behavior, how to help him or her understand the ethical demands of the purchasing function in your company, and how to help people live up to their principles. Most people want to do the right thing. They want to do their work by the same set of standards they live by. For example, a recent Illinois Institute of Technology study found that the great majority of people will not accept large gifts or favors from suppliers. Even food and liquor are *only actually accepted by 9%* of purchasing professionals even though 29% think this is acceptable. Large favors such as vacation trips and automobiles are only actually accepted less than 1% of the time. Similar results were found for Christmas gifts. Small gifts with a value up to $10 were considered acceptable by roughly one-quarter of the professionals surveyed. Is a round of golf at the best country club on a Friday afternoon acceptable? When the gift was over $100, the acceptable rate fell to 0.4%. Your role as a purchasing professional is to nurture and grow these natural tendencies by:

- recognizing good work.
- dealing fairly with all employees.
- conducting a rigorous interview process.
- making sure that personalities fit.
- doing what you say.

For example, you should let both buyers and sales representatives know that they must be up front in their negotiations. Tell them that delivery, quality, service and price must be clearly stated. And, above all, let them know that they must always treat their counterparts with respect.

Team Spirit

Ethical behavior thrives in an open and egalitarian environment, a place in which collegial relationships and teamwork are encouraged. Teamwork, itself, is the result of a process of people involvement/empowerment. Each of the following consequences, all of them working in a dynamic conjunction, are the material from which you can fashion a viable ethics program.

- Create a stronger and more effective ethics foundation
- A network of improved communication by examples

- An environment safe for discussions

Quite clearly, people foster ethical behavior by accepting responsibility. The more responsibility given to the individual, the more he or she feels that he/she has ownership. This creates a sense of bonding in which people work to gain the admiration of their fellow workers and to avoid the shame of acting against the group's interests. Case study models show how ethics work. Lastly, the task-oriented nature of teams helps make ethical problems more concrete and less abstract.

Ethics and Performance Evaluation

Based on the importance of ethics in promoting ethical behavior, we have found that an excellent way to evaluate your ethics program is to measure its effectiveness with an audit, internal or external. This information would give management a capsule overview of how adherence in the workplace has become.

Ethical behavior also flourishes in an environment in which people are given positive encouragement when they are being evaluated for their performance. We are not advocating that constructive criticism be eliminated; it still has its place. What we are saying is that you shouldn't wait for something to go wrong to inform people about their performance. And we are also saying that positive encouragement is not as simple as giving a person a pat on the back. There are ways of encouraging people that are far more effective than others. Here are some of the guidelines we have found most important in our work:

- **Be specific.** Like criticism, praise should state exactly what behavior is being rewarded. General praise is bad for two reasons. It doesn't specify what needs to be reinforced and it often comes across as insincere.

- **Be immediate.** Give praise as soon after the desired behavior as possible. An informal thank you in the hallway five minutes later is more effective than a formal handshake two weeks later.

- **Don't mix praise with criticism.** Doing this gives the person a mixed message and dilutes the power of both messages. If you mix the two, the person only waits for the bad news.

- **Don't overuse praise.** Overused praise loses its value and effectiveness.

Ethics and Hiring

A company cannot rely on people who have become part of the corporate culture when the need to hire people from outside the company exists. It can present problems for validating the individual's ethical background. One of the best ways, however, to be sure of hiring people with integrity is to have the reputation of being a highly ethical company. When considering what people to hire, don't let their intelligence, record (economic performance), and energy blind you to their character. All require a background check and should sign a statement attesting that their credentials are correct. We have found that there are four types of workers. Those who:

1) deliver on commitment and share values.

2) do not deliver on commitment or share values.

3) do not deliver on commitment but share values.

4) deliver on commitments but do not share values.

Clearly, the first type is the best. The worker described in #4 may have the intelligence, performance record and energy discussed above, but if he or she does not share your company's values, there is the potential for problems in the future. We must hire the best people available and pay them their worth. Unethical people lower the morale of their fellow workers when a company is perceived as not practicing what it preaches. We would also like to add that these guidelines apply to the hiring of consultants, accountants, lawyers, and all people involved in your business.

Conducting Ethics Surveys

Chances are good that you already have some form of an ethics program in your department, which ideally evolved from the broader, corporate policy. But how effective is your departmental program? Do you need to alter your ethical reputation?

Ethics surveys are very useful in the validation of an ethics program at your company. They can be used as a baseline to track change as well as to determine what's going on now. We advocate that you use focus groups or surveys to find out what ethics issues are of concern to workers. Part of the process of fostering an ethical company culture is taken up by people surveys which measure the strengths, weaknesses and needs of the organization's people. Collecting meaningful and accurate data is the result of careful planning and testing of a survey prior to its being given to an entire organization.

TEN STEPS FOR DESIGNING A SURVEY

STEP ONE: Define Goals. Describe the desired outcome of the survey. What kind of data will be obtained by this survey? In order to pinpoint what is to be accomplished by a survey, begin by establishing priorities.

STEP TWO: Target the Group. Who is the group from which the data will be gathered? Will it be one segment of the organization such as those directly involved with production, or will the target group be everyone in the organization? The answer to this question is determined by the goals that you have defined above.

STEP THREE: Determine the Survey Sample. It is often unrealistic to survey everyone in the target group because it contains too many members. The solution is to take a representative portion of the target group and extrapolate conclusions from the results of the survey sample.

STEP FOUR: Develop the Questionnaire. A comprehensive survey must contain four parts. They are:

- A cover letter — Should clearly state the purpose of the survey, how results will be used and when they will be shared as well as guarantee the anonymity of the respondent.

- The items (questions or statements) — Should also be clear and to the point. Make sure each item asks only one question or addresses only one issue so that there is no ambiguity. Word them so that any bias is removed. Don't use language that could be interpreted as a threat to the people taking the survey.

- The scales — Should range from strong positive feelings to strong negative feelings.

- The codes — Should indicate how to handle problem responses or no response to an item. It should also indicate the score, or point value, of each item.

STEP FIVE: Pretest the Questionnaire. In order to fine tune the questionnaire, pretest a small group from those people who will be surveyed. Examine the results to determine whether the responses are skewed or whether they are balanced on either side of the issue.

STEP SIX: Prepare the Final Draft. Correct any problems identified in the previous step and prepare an easy-to-read final draft.

STEP SEVEN: Administer the Questionnaire. Distribute the cover letter and questionnaire to all that will participate within the targeted group. Define a time frame for completion of the survey and give precise directions for turning it in.

STEP EIGHT: Code the Responses. Create a coding system that identifies the origin of the responses. Factors to consider coding include: department, sex, position in organization, age and any other factor which might add value to the survey results or identify bias in the design of the survey.

STEP NINE: Tabulate the Results. Transfer the information from each completed survey to a master which compiles the results of all the surveys.

STEP TEN: Prepare the Report. Analyze the results of the survey tabulation. Are any trends revealed? Does there seem to be a common attitude that exists among those surveyed? Does the survey point out specific areas of opportunity where improvements can be effected?

Feedback, often overlooked in this step, illustrates that you are serious about the ethics. As we have mentioned, ethics programs are most effective when you practice what you preach.

ETHICS IN
EVERYDAY
SITUATIONS

CHAPTER EIGHT

Purchasing ethics is not something that companies should think about every now and then. Ethics is an everyday activity that must be based on established principles. There are some sociologists who believe that this base is eroding in our society. A recent report by the Internal Revenue Service, for example, says that 50% of us believe it is acceptable to be a bit dishonest in our dealings with large companies. Of course, some companies are as much as fault in this perceived erosion of ethical principles as evidenced by such activities as illegal dumping of hazardous materials or evading full payment of taxes. Our purpose here is not to parcel out blame, but to ask all purchasing professionals to raise their level of awareness concerning ethical issues. We have done this in the professional arena throughout this book, but let's now turn briefly to the ethics of the individual in everyday situations. This will, we hope, put the professional ethical issues raised elsewhere in this book into an accessible context.

19th century politician and historian Babington Macauley stated, "The measure of a man's real character is what he would do if he knew he would never be found out." The quiz below can be used to give you an idea about the ethical tone of the individual. Take a few minutes to complete the questions. Then, add up your score to see where you stand.

1) It is okay for an individual to decide what is right and wrong instead of following the rules of society as long as he or she causes no harm to another person.

   Regarding this statement, are you:

   A In complete agreement?

   B In agreement?

   C In disagreement?

   D In complete disagreement?

2) A friend who has just got a promotion tells you that he "beefed up" his resume a bit by indicating that he received a higher degree than he actually obtained and that he had a higher salary than he actually earned. "Everybody does it," he says. "If you don't, you'll never move ahead."

   What do you think of his advice?

   A In complete agreement

B In agreement

C In disagreement

3 **D** In complete disagreement

3) You rent a car with a full tank of gas. When you return the car, the agent asks if you bought gas for the car and if the car has a full tank. You know that you have used some of the gas, even though the gauge still reads full.

Would you tell the clerk the gas tank is full?

A Definitely would

1 **B** Probably would

C Probably wouldn't

D Definitely wouldn't

4) You have submitted your monthly expense report and by some oversight, accounting has sent you two checks. You put the extra check in a file to return, but forget about it. Two months later, you discover the check and realize that nobody will discover the error.

Do you cash the check?

A Without a doubt

B Probably would do it

C Would consider it

3 **D** Absolutely not

5) You are in a car accident that causes $3,000 worth of damage to your automobile. Your deductible is $500, but the adjuster suggests that he will

say there was $4,000 worth of damage if you "share" the difference with him?

Do you take him up on his suggestion?

A Certainly

B Probably, but with second thoughts

2 **C** Probably not, but I could use the money

D Not at all

6) Your spouse is working hard to pass a licensing exam. He has been working full-time and going to school at night. He learns that several students have a stolen copy of the exam and that he can buy a copy for $200.

What do you advise him to do?

A Buy the exam

B Buy it because everybody else is

C Don't buy it, but question if that is the most
3 practical advice

D Say "thanks, but no thanks" and study harder

7) You're buying food and supplies for the family picnic. While you are checking out, the clerk gets distracted and forgets to ring up about $100 worth of ribs and chicken wings. He totals the bill.

Do you say nothing and walk out of the store?

A Absolutely

3 **B** Probably

C Probably not

D Definitely not

8) You've just got married and are moving into a new apartment with your spouse. All of your utility and telephone accounts are in your old roommate's name because you never bothered to change them over. You realize that if you put the new accounts in your spouse's name, you won't have to pay all the old bills since they will be looking for your roommate who moved out of state.

Do you skip out on paying the old bills?

3

A Of course

B Maybe

C No, probably too risky

(**D**)No way

9) You do some free-lance consulting in your field. One steady client wants to pay you less and suggests that if you accepted cash, you would not have to report the income on your tax return. They would like you to cut your fees by a percentage of what you gain by not reporting.

Do you go along with them?

A In a blink of an eye

3

B Why not?

C I don't think so.

(**D**)Tell them that you definitely won't

10) You own a warehouse in an industrial park of a city that has hit some hard times. You can't sell or rent the building and have been trying for several years. A few other warehouses in the park have burned down. You know that it wasn't vandals,

but the companies have collected on insurance. You think you know a way that you can get rid of your building with nobody knowing the better by blaming it on the vandals that nobody has caught.

If you could get away with it, would you have somebody commit arson?

A Absolutely

B Probably

3   **C** Probably not

   Ⓓ Definitely not

Now, score the quiz according to the following point values:

A	0
B	1
C	2
D	3

Take your total score and see how you rate:

27-30   An honest individual whose ethics are in line with society

19-26   Generally honest, but susceptible to temptation

9-18   Mostly dishonest; seeking personal gain with occasional tinges of conscience

0-8   Dishonest; at odds with established societal ethics

Now let's look at what you can do to help get your company on a path to ethical behavior within your profession. The two case studies that follow should also aid you in shaping your purchasing department's ethics.

Case Study #1: Justifying Policies to Top Management

Your boss has just spent the last hour telling you how the president of your company was called before the board of directors and grilled about the latest purchasing scandals in your industry. Even though the president assured the board that your company does not engage in price fixing, collusion, payola, excessive business gifts, or conflicts of interest, they wanted to know what the purchasing department was doing to assure that it would not happen there. The president demanded an action plan from your boss and now she is demanding that you draw up some guidelines. How do you convince the board that you are getting the lowest total cost from your suppliers on an ethical basis? What would be the basis of your action plan? Here is what we would suggest:

Action Items

- Examine and review existing company standards.
- Set up standards in areas lacking them.
- Seek legal counsel when needed.
- Educate self and others.
- Avoid the appearance of unethical behavior.

Around these basic action items and with the material presented in this book, you should be able to start the process of convincing not only the board, but your customers and suppliers, that you conduct your purchasing activities in a fair and ethical manner.

Case Study #2: Conflict of Interest

Betty Brown, purchasing director for the XYZ Company, finds out that one of her buyers, Bill White, is buying technical support services for the company's CAD/CAM system from a software development company different from the original developer. That is not a problem since the original developer has gone out of business and the new supplier is known as one of the best in the business. The problem is that the vice-president of development at the new software company is Bob White, the brother of Bill. Upon further investigation, it turns out that Bill was discussing the problem of finding technical support with his brother who told Bill that his company had taken over the support services for a number of old clients of the original developer.

"I'll have someone send you some information on what we do and what we charge," Bob told Bill.

When Bill received the information, he checked it against competitors and discovered that the company his brother worked for provided the lowest total cost for this type of support service. And their quality was second to none. Bill also told Betty that XYZ Company had saved over $135,000 a quarter for the past three quarters by using the company where Bob worked.

"I can't tell you how many shutdowns and crashes we have avoided because of their expertise," Bill told Betty. "Everybody in the business says they are the best."

At first Betty believed that Bill had conducted himself well, but she began to have doubts. She talked to the company's legal counsel who said that Bill should be fired for conspiracy to defraud the company.

"You've got to nip this in the bud," he emphatically told her.

Betty's colleague, the R&D manager, strongly disagreed. "I know Bob and the company he works for. They are above reproach. Bill did what was best for our company by selecting them as a supplier."

Who is right in this situation? What would you do if you were Betty?

_____

_____

_____

_____

_____

The fault here seems to be that there is no clear policy on conflict of interest that Bill could have consulted before he contracted with the company his brother works for. In the absence of a policy, he cannot be entirely faulted for what he did. On the other hand, Bill could have used some prudence and alerted Betty to the potential of a conflict when he first received the information about the new supplier. Betty could have then given the buying responsibilities to somebody else in the Purchasing Department or asked for guidance from the company's legal counsel or from her boss. This case study is a good example of what can happen if ethical guidelines are not spelled out.

Ethical and Policy Dimensions of Purchasing Practices

We leave you with one important piece of advice. Honest people can and will differ over what is and isn't an ethical purchasing practice. Whereas most purchasing professionals, for example, believe that it is acceptable to use their company's buying power to obtain price concessions and favorable service, there are some who believe this practice is unacceptable. On the other hand, it is almost unanimous among purchasing professionals that allowing one supplier to see another supplier's quotation and to resubmit a bid is unethical. Whatever the difference there may be concerning the ethics of a particular behavior, purchasing professionals are in agreement that there needs to be a stated policy for each and every purchasing practice. The following list of purchasing practices requiring such a policy statement, although extensive, can never be complete. It is your responsibility as a purchasing professional to know where in your company and department needs reinforcement.

The following purchasing practices should be evaluated by purchasing managers in order to write a policy statement:

1. Accepting gifts such as sales promotion prizes or "purchase-volume incentive bonuses."

2. Permitting a supplier to see a competitor's quotation or providing information about a supplier's competitor.

3. Accepting free trips, free luncheons or dinners, or other free entertainment that is outside normal business practices.

4. Providing suppliers who are good customers with special treatment.

5. Exaggerating problems with an existing supplier in order to get better prices or obtain other concessions.

6. Providing better treatment to suppliers that your company's managers or executives prefer or recommend.

7. Showing bias against suppliers whose salespeople circumvent the purchasing department.

8. Soliciting quotations from new suppliers even though current supplier selection process heavily favors existing suppliers.

9. Asking a supplier to cancel a purchase order for parts already in production as well as waiving cancellation charges.

10. Basing the supplier selection process on personality.

11. Obtaining price or other concessions from suppliers based on your firm's buying power.

12. Informing an existing supplier that you are gathering information for a second source so that the original supplier will lower its price or grant other concessions.

13. Asking your suppliers for information about your competitors.

As you have learned from this book, purchasing ethics is not a one-shot deal in which you draw up a list of rules. Situations always come up in which the old rules do not apply. That is why the professional purchasing manager places a high emphasis on making the rules a way of life. We have written this book to help you do that job. The time to start this process is now.

ADDITIONAL PURCHASING RESOURCES
FROM PT PUBLICATIONS, INC.

3109 45th Street, Suite 100
West Palm Beach, FL 33407-1915
1-800-547-4326

THE PURCHASING ENCYCLOPEDIA

Just-In-Time Purchasing: In Pursuit of Excellence $29.95
   Peter L. Grieco, Jr., Michael W. Gozzo
   & Jerry W. Claunch

Glossary of Key Purchasing Terms, Acronyms, *and Formulas* PT Publications	$14.95
Supplier Certification II: A Handbook for *Achieving Excellence through Continuous Improvement* Peter L. Grieco, Jr.	$49.95
World Class: Measuring Its Achievement Peter L. Grieco, Jr.	$39.95
Purchasing Performance Measurements: A Roadmap *For Excellence* Mel Pilachowski	$12.95
The World Of Negotiations: Never Being a Loser Peter L. Grieco, Jr. and Paul G. Hine	$39.95
How To Conduct Supplier Surveys and Audits Janet L. Przirembel	$14.95
Supply Management Toolbox: How to Manage *Your Suppliers* Peter L. Grieco, Jr.	$26.95
Purchasing Capital Equipment Wayne L. Douchkoff	$14.95
Power Purchasing: Supply Management in *in the 21st Century* Peter L. Grieco, Jr. and Carl R. Cooper	$39.95
Global Sourcing Lee Krotseng	$14.95
Purchasing Contract Law, UCC, and Patents Mark Grieco	$14.95
EDI Purchasing: The Electronic Gateway *to the Future* Steven Marks	$14.95
Leasing Smart Craig A. Melby and Jane Utzman	$14.95
MRO Purchasing Peter L. Grieco, Jr.	$14.95
Purchasing Transportation Charles L. Perry	$14.95

The Complete Guide to Contracts Management For	$18.95
Facilities Services	
John P. Mahoney and Linda S. Keckler	
Purchasing Ethics	$14.95
Peter L. Grieco, Jr.	
Procurement Reengineering	$14.95
Ben H. Laaper	
Supplier Strategies	$14.95
Charles Goldfeld	
Supplier Selection	$14.95
Judith A. Stimson	
Supply Chain Management	$14.95
Peter L. Grieco, Jr. and John Gossmann	

PURCHASING VIDEO EDUCATION SERIES

Supplier Certification The Path to Excellence	
Tape 1: Why Supplier Certification?	$395.00
Tape 2: Quality at the Supplier	$395.00
Tape 3: How to Select a Supplier	$395.00
Tape 4: Supplier Surveys and Audits	$395.00
Tape 5: Supplier Quality Agreements	$395.00
Tape 6: Supplier Ratings	$395.00
Tape 7: Phases of Supplier Certification	$395.00
Tape 8: Implementing a Supplier Cert. Program	$395.00
Tape 9: Evaluating Your Supplier Cert. Program	$395.00
Complete Nine Tape Series	$1,995.00

PURCHASING AUDIO TAPES

The World of Negotiations: How to Win Every Time	$39.95

PURCHASING SOFTWARE

Supplier Survey and Audit Software $395.00
     Developed by Professionals For Technology, Inc.

ADDITIONAL PROFESSIONAL TEXTBOOKS

Failure Modes and Effects Analysis: Predicting $39.95
     and Preventing Problems Before They Occur
     Paul Palady
Made In America: The Total Business Concept $29.95
     Peter L. Grieco, Jr. and Michael W. Gozzo
Reengineering Through Cycle Time Management $39.95
     Wayne L. Douchkoff and Thomas E. Petroski
Behind Bars: Bar Coding Principles and Applications $39.95
     Peter L. Grieco, Jr., Michael W. Gozzo and C. J. Long
People Empowerment: Achieving Success from Involvement $39.95
     Michael W. Gozzo and Wayne L. Douchkoff
Activity Based Costing: The Key to World Class Performance $18.00
     Peter L. Grieco, Jr. and Mel Pilachowski
Set-Up Reduction: The Next Millennium $26.95
     Thomas E. Petroski

INDEX